There are Stranger Stars

by

W.B. Clark

There are Stranger Stars

ISBN: 979-8-9865649-1-3

Copyright © 2023 by W.B. Clark

All rights reserved.

www.wbclarkbooks.com

For all the adults who still dream of Magic

There are stranger stars out there

go find them

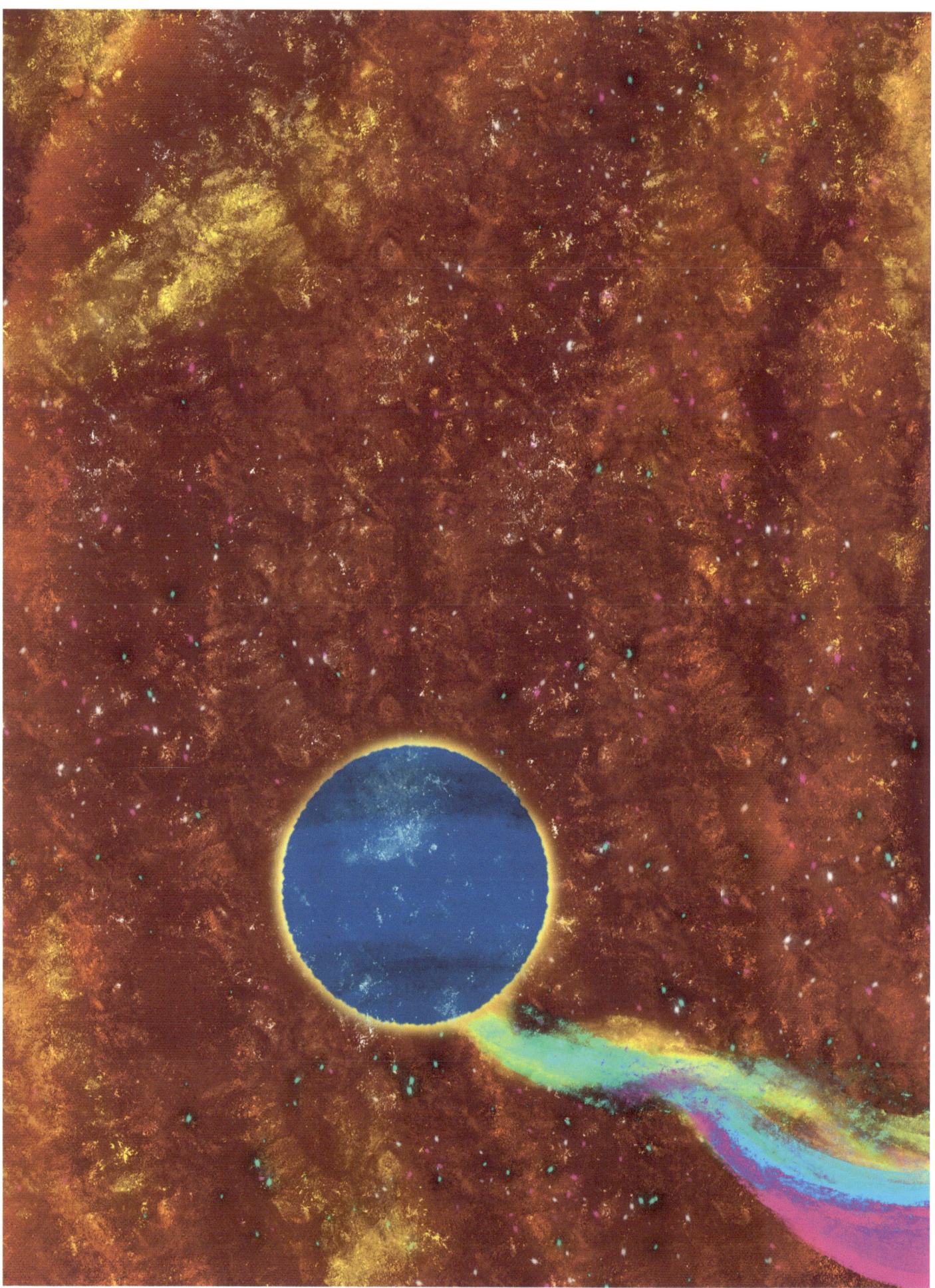

The light can shine brilliantly
yet darkness can still creep in
You can have everything in the universe
and still feel sorrow
Nonetheless
You are a beacon
So even if your base is cracked
and your soul weary
take a rest
then stand again

I wondered where
my soul went
amidst the heartache
little did I know

my light was here
the entire time

I get to be right here

Found You

Thank you for reading!

For additional books & art by W.B. Clark,

visit: www.wbclarkbooks.com

Adult Titles:

A Thousand Short Lives

Future Adult Titles:

Giving Up Elysium

Heart of Áides

For Children:

So You Want to Be a Witch?

ABOUT THE AUTHOR

W.B. Clark is from small-town Oklahoma, mostly raised on a farm full of chickens and then partially on a boat in Alaska. She graduated from the University of Oklahoma, then moved to some big cities, where life happened. She finally got a job that pays her bills, and sometimes, she gets to write books and illustrate pretty pictures on the side. In between, she plays random instruments poorly, swears often, and wonders where her next adventure will be. Some of which involve hiking, camping, scuba diving, and starting complex projects she knows little to nothing about. She loves breakfast, good friends, and hearing other people's stories.

www.ingramcontent.com/pod-product-compliance
Lightning Source LLC
Chambersburg PA
CBHW040728060526
44119CB00084B/356

For those who have passed on, and those who are yet to come; inspired by our "joy in June" Channing and my beloved one Cavaughn.

I Am Well

Mantras for young hearts and young minds

Author
Iana Del Darlington Jordan Benjamin

Illustrator
Jeanine-Jonee

All rights reserved. This book or parts thereof may not be reproduced in any form, stored in any retrieval system, or transmitted in any form by any means—electronic, mechanical, photocopy, recording, or otherwise—without prior written permission of the publisher, except as provided by United States of America copyright law.

For permission requests write to the publisher, addressed "Attention: Permissions Coordinator," at the address below.

Printing in the United States of America 1st Printing

ISBN
979-8-9863173-0-4

Library of Congress
TXu 2-320-232

Author Website
Darlingtonjordanlaw.com

Disclaimer
This publication is meant as a source of valuable information for the reader, however it is not meant as a substitute for direct expert assistance. If such level of assistance is required, the services of a competent professional should be sought.

I am well.
I am flowing like the ocean.
I am flowing like the streams.

I am well.
I am rustling like the cane fields.
I am rustling like the trees.

I am well.
I am soaring high in the clouds.
I am soaring like the eagles above.

I am well.
I am enough.
I am made of good stuff.

I am well.
I am the source of all goodness.
I am the source of kindness.

*I am well.
I am grace.
I am fit to run and win this race.*

I am well.
I represent blessings from above.
I am mercy, I am love.

Iana Del Darlington Jordan Benjamin

is a Family Law Litigator, specializing in assisting families with Domestic Litigation. She is also a Adjunct Professor of Ethics, Law and Special Topics in Pre-Law at Edward Waters University. Iana has more than a decade of years of insights experience working with students, children, families to solve and resolve their most important challenges and conflicts.

Iana is a native of the beautiful twin island nation of Trinidad & Tobago. Iana currently lives in Germany with her husband and young son.

Jeanine-Jonee
Also known as 'Jenjo'

An illustrator who primarily works on children's books and comics. She's the creator, writer and illustrator of the all age series "Seafoam: A Friend for Madison".

Jeanine-Jonee is a Cherokee Citizen who resides in Southern California. Alongside her illustrative work, she coordinates specialty art classes for kids, which includes teaching children how to write their own children's books, and draw their own comics.

If you'd like to view some of her other artworks, they can be found on her website.

jenjoink.com

Craft/Write/Create Your Own Mantras

Craft/Write/Create Your Own Mantras

AM

WELL

www.ingramcontent.com/pod-product-compliance
Lightning Source LLC
Chambersburg PA
CBHW040728060526
44119CB00084B/357